Louis Zangwill

The beautiful Miss Brooke

Louis Zangwill

The beautiful Miss Brooke

ISBN/EAN: 9783337138769

Printed in Europe, USA, Canada, Australia, Japan

Cover: Foto ©ninafisch / pixelio.de

More available books at **www.hansebooks.com**

THE BEAUTIFUL MISS BROOKE

The Beautiful Miss Brooke

By "Z. Z."
Author of A Drama in Dutch,
The World and a Man, Etc.

New York
D. Appleton and Company
1897

COPYRIGHT, 1897,
D. APPLETON AND COMPANY.

THE BEAUTIFUL MISS BROOKE.

CHAPTER I.

THE opening bars of a waltz sounded through the house above the irregular murmur of conversation, bearing their promise and summons along festal corridors and into garlanded nooks and alcoves. Paul Middleton drew a breath of relief as the girl to whom he had been talking was carried off to dance, for she had bored him intolerably. The refreshment room, crowded a moment ago, was thinning down, and, glad of the respite, he took another sandwich and slowly sipped the remainder of his coffee. His humour was of the worst. If his hostess had not been his mother's oldest friend, he would never have allowed himself to be persuaded to accept her invitation after he had once decided to decline it. Why had his mother so persisted, when she knew very well he was looking forward to playing in an important chess match? Certainly the evening so far had not compensated him for the pleasure he had thus missed.

He had been chafing the whole time, and intermittently he had played with the idea of slipping out and taking a hansom down to the chess club. But he had ticked off five dances on Celia's programme—Celia was of course Celia—and he was to take her to supper. Moreover, on his arrival at the small-and-early, Mrs. Saxon had led him round—he feeling that his amiable expression made him a hypocrite—and, mechanically repeating his request for the pleasure of a dance, he had scrawled his name on several programmes with scarcely a glance at their owners. It was, however, more particularly his engagements with Celia, and one or two other girls he knew well, that had made him stay on. Once more he glanced at his watch. It was getting well on towards midnight now, and the issue of the chess match must already have been decided. After some speculation as to the winning side, he resigned himself to finishing the evening where he was.

At the best of times Paul Middleton's interest in the ballroom was only lukewarm. He frankly professed not to care about it at all, and, though he was in the habit of dancing every dance, he looked upon himself more as a spectator than a participator on such rare occasions as he accepted cards for. He had no favourite partners. Into the inner and intimate life of that circle of light made for human pleasure he could never enter; he had always shrunk from exploring its labyrinth of flirtation, coquetry, and petty manœuvring, the very thought of the intricacies of which affrighted his plain-sailing temperament. To him one girl in a ballroom was much the same as another—a green, white, or pink gown with sometimes an eye-glass attached. He knew very well, though—if only from his mother having instilled it into him—that no such indifference attached to him, a young man of twenty-three, who was absolute master of at least eleven thousand pounds a year, and not without claim to other merits.

Becoming aware that the music was in full swing upstairs, he began to think it was high time to look for his partner. But the name "Brooke" on his programme, which he made out with some difficulty, called up no picture, no living personality. He could not even recollect the moment when he had written it, and it did not appear he had made any note to help him identify the girl. His last partner had had to be pointed out to him by Mrs. Saxon, and he did not care to trouble her again. "Besides," he reflected, "this Miss Brooke, whoever she is, will most likely be hidden away in some nook or other and will be only too glad not to be hunted up."

He had almost made up his mind to skip the dance when there came into the room an old schoolfellow, more or less a friend of his. The two interchanged a word. Thorn, it appeared, wanted a whisky and soda before going home. He had to turn in early to be in good form for the morrow's cricket. It was the first match of the season, and he was anxious to do brilliantly. Paul took the opportunity of asking him if, by any chance, he knew or had danced with a Miss Brooke.

"The beautiful Miss Brooke you mean, don't you?" asked Thorn.

Paul explained he didn't know which Miss Brooke he meant, but that he ought to be dancing with *a* Miss Brooke. Any girl who answered to that name would satisfy him.

"Well, if the one you mean, or don't mean, is the one I mean, she's just outside the door talking to a big Yankee chap. I never heard of her before to-night, but she's a stunning girl. She's the daughter of some American millionaire, a railway king, or something of that sort—at least everybody says so. I tried to get a dance with her, but I wasn't in luck. I envy you. Good-night, old boy!"

"I suppose, then, *I* must consider myself in luck," thought Paul, staying yet a moment as he caught sight of his full reflection in a glass. It was a medium, slightly built figure that met his gaze, easy and graceful of carriage. The face was fair with a tiny light beard—the silken hair cut short, the features intelligent, the eyes grey, the teeth beautiful. A suspicion of a freckle here and there did not seem unsuited to the type of complexion. The survey seemed to please him, and he stepped forward with the intention of taking possession of "the beautiful Miss Brooke."

Thorn's indication proved correct. To his surprise Miss Brooke seemed to recognise him as he approached, for she welcomed him with a smile, from which he deduced, moreover, that she must have been waiting for him. He had a general sense of enchantment and diaphanousness, of a delicate harmony of colour-tones; an impression as of an idealised figure that had stepped out of a decorative painting. He wondered how he had escaped the impression at the time of his introduction to her, and, despite her smile, he was chilled by a doubt that it might, after all, be some other Miss Brooke on whose programme he had written. Of the man she had been talking to he scarcely took any note at all, beyond verifying he was a "big Yankee." He took her up to the dancing-room, and they began waltzing. Paul considered himself a pretty good dancer, and there were even moments when he could conscientiously say he was enjoying himself. But somehow he found himself going badly with Miss Brooke. Things seemed to be wrong at the very start. There was an uncomfortable drag. Paul was compelled to take enormous steps to counteract it, and after a dozen turns both agreed to give it up.

"You dance the English step, of course, Mr. Middleton," she observed as they sauntered round. Her American accent was of the slightest, and few as were the words she had so far spoken, they seemed to Paul subtly to vibrate with a pleasant friendliness. Her voice was sweet and clear, with an under-quality of softness and caress. The suggestion that there were waltz steps other than the one he was wont to dance was new to him.

"I suppose mine is the English step," he

replied, "though I never heard of any other. Is yours very different?"

"Oh, yes. We Americans really waltz, whilst you English just go round and round and round, with your stiff legs for all the world like a pair of compasses."

Paul could not agree with her, and patriotically proceeded to defend the English waltz, surprised to find himself expending oratory on so trivial a subject. He asserted it was not the mere monotonous turning to which Miss Brooke would reduce it, but that a spirit went with it; whereupon Miss Brooke shook her head, declaring she had shown the American step to a good many English people, and, no matter how sceptical before, they had vowed, one and all, never to dance the English step again.

They had wandered away from the mass of rotating figures and taken possession of a couple of seats in a corner outside the dancing-room. Paul had now an opportunity of observing Miss Brooke more narrowly. Other partners he had already forgotten. He could hardly have identified them again. So far as he was concerned, they had got completely lost in the crowd from which they had temporarily emerged. But of Miss Brooke he felt sure a perfectly definite picture would remain in his mind. What struck him most at once was a certain spirit of frank good humour that seemed to exhale from her, that made him feel, even with her first few words, as if she were merely resuming an interrupted conversation with him. Her manner suggested the natural falling-into-step by the side of an established friend, overtaken *en route,* and it was hard for him to realise this was really their first talk together.

Paul had never danced with an American girl before, else he would have been aware of the incompatibility of their steps. His notions of the American girl—or at least the American girl that comes to Europe—were of the vaguest. He had in the course of his existence met perhaps two or three of the class, but he had never really talked to them. He had heard the American girl spoken of—praised, damned, or tolerated; he had read about her push and businesslike qualities; and a short time since he had seen the type portrayed on the stage—a dashing, masterful creature, a piece of egotism incarnate, with a twang as pronounced as her self-assertiveness, a terrible determination, and an equally terrible assurance of carrying it through. But he had never thought about her coherently; never consciously crystallized these more or less contradictory notions of her that had come to him in so scattered and chaotic a fashion. It was quite certain, however, that Miss Brooke had nothing in common with the monstrosity that had given so much delight to that English audience, and raised in it a due consciousness of its own virtue of modest moderation. Nor could he associate her with the dreadfully improper and unabashable person he had heard more than one British matron declare the American girl to be.

Miss Brooke did not address her words to the floor, but sitting with her chair at an angle to his, looking straight at him as she spoke. Paul found the ordeal a fascinating but sufficiently trying one. He had no chance against this wonderful girlish face, with its sparkling blue eyes and its subtle quality of sincerity and spirituality; tantalising by the charm of its smile, which suggested moments of wickedness and kissing, and provoking by its air of unawareness of its calm-destroying powers. He was conscious, too, of a long, white neck rising above a pair of well-knit shoulders, out of a mass of white fluffy trimmings, in which were set with careless art a few deep-red velvet flowers. On her forehead lay two roguish curls that moved freely, and each temple was covered by a bewitching lock, whose end curled inwards toward the ear. At the back her hair was drawn right up into curls, leaving the whole neck free, and showing the contour of the gracefully-poised head. Her white gown seemed woven of some fairy substance, embroidered with myriad gold spots, and encircled round the waist with three golden bands. The pink, round flesh of the upper arm showed firm and cool through the web of the sleeve that met the long white glove at the elbow. The bodice followed closely the modelling of the bust, and the skirt swept downwards, ending in a mass of foam-like fluff amid which nestled the tips of two neat shoes. Altogether a superb girl, dainty and supple, without any suggestion of fragility.

The comparative merits of the English and

American waltzes were still occupying their attention.

"Now, tell me, Mr. Middleton," she asked, after enthusiastically descanting on the pleasure and grace of the "long glide," "haven't I really converted you?"

"I want very much to be converted, but your waltz seems formidable. I am afraid of it."

"I'm sure it would not take you long to learn. Cannot I really coax you into a promise to try it? I enjoy making converts—I have missionary tendencies in the blood."

"That's interesting. Because there are tendencies in my blood, too. Anti-missionary ones, however. To be true to the family tradition, I'm not sure whether I ought not resist your coaxings."

"Which I'm sure you're not going to do." Her face took on an expression of mock imploration. "But, tell me, how far back does your tradition go, and how did it arise?"

"It began with my grandfather, whose pet idea was that the energy and money spent on missions should be employed at home for the raising of the lower classes. My father went a step further by deciding the particular form in which the lower classes should reap the benefit, and he died with the hope that the dream of two generations should be realised by me."

"There is quite a touch of poetry in what you tell me," said Miss Brooke. "My family history is more prosaic, but it has a dash of adventure in it. The missionary hobby began with my great-grandfather, who was devoted, body and soul, to it—certainly body, for he was eaten by cannibals. Poor savages!"

"Poor savages!" echoed Paul, for the moment supposing Miss Brooke meant to throw doubts on her ancestor's digestibility.

"Yes, for grandfather went out to preach to them! A very mean revenge, I call that."

"How do you reconcile that statement with your own missionary leanings?" asked Paul, thinking it strange a railway king should be the son of an earnest missionary, and vaguely speculating whether the millionaire was in the habit of giving large sums to "revenge" his grandfather.

"Oh, as a woman I have the right to make contradictory statements. 'Tis a valuable right, and I find it very convenient not to yield it up, though I *did* learn logic at college."

"But surely it must be ever so much nicer to triumph by logic."

"If one were only sure of triumphing! But I am really in no difficulty, so you will not get an exhibition of logic to-night. My missionary tendencies are purely a matter of instinct, my anti-missionary ones a matter of sentiment. Do not instinct and sentiment pull different ways in human beings? Confess, Mr. Middleton, don't you often *want* to do things you *feel* you ought not?"

"More often I don't want to do things I feel I ought to."

"That is a piece of new humour."

"I meant the inversion seriously. But I'm glad to find that we are agreed at least in sentiment."

"And I do try and turn the instinct into useful channels. Americans, you know, never let force run to waste. Now, you *will* learn that waltz, won't you, Mr. Middleton? Promise me quickly, as some one is coming to take me to dance. There comes the top of his head."

"Dear me, has the next dance come round already!" ejaculated Paul. "You may consider me a sincere convert," he added quickly, "if—if you will spare me another dance."

"If you can find one," she replied; and, slipping her programme into his hand, she rose in response to the smile of the new-comer. To Paul's surprise, the man was the same from whom he had carried off Miss Brooke only a minute or two ago, as it appeared to him. Which fact caused him now to take keen notice of him. "The fellow" was quite six feet high, and of slim, supple build. His face was dark, and, to Paul, distinctively American. He wore a short pointed beard and a carefully-trimmed moustache. His black hair somewhat eccentrically hung down in lines cut to the same length. His eyes gleamed with an almost unnatural brightness, and his teeth showed themselves polished and white.

"Write thick over somebody else's name." Paul was conscious of Miss Brooke speaking to him in almost a whisper; then in a moment she had bowed and moved off. He could not help feeling angry with the man for taking her away, and his displeasure showed itself in his face. There seemed, too, something proprietorial in the way "the confounded fellow" walked off with her, and a thousand foolish conjectures hustled in his brain. However, he remembered he had Miss Brooke's programme, which, together with her last injunction, formed a comforting assurance she had taken him into special favour. It had been decidedly nice to talk to this girl, who seemed just the sort of person—simple and straightforward despite her wonderful charm—he felt he could get on with, and it gave him pleasure to picture her again sitting by his side, fresh, cool, sweet, and surpassingly beautiful.

After lingering a little he went into the ballroom again. Miss Brooke's figure alone drew his eye—the rest of the world was a mere dancing medley. She was obviously enjoying her dance, and Paul found himself envying her partner his easy mastery of the American waltz step. He could not help observing now what a superb note she struck in that crowd. He could see, too, she was being noticed, and divined talk about her by many moving lips.

He found an opportunity of returning her programme, which she received with a marked look of surprise that changed into a smile of thanks. Paul was much puzzled. Her manner seemed to make it appear that she had dropped the programme and he had picked it up. He rather resented this, till it occurred to him she had slipped it into his hand so as not to be seen by her present cavalier, and probably she had played this little comedy because she did not want to rouse his suspicion. Paul's fears that the man might be something to her were re-awakened, but they were palliated by a sense of triumph over him. Had not Miss Brooke played a part—for his sake?

Mrs. Saxon passed near him and stopped to talk to him a moment. He made absent-minded replies—indeed, five minutes later he recalled that he had said something particularly foolish and hated himself. In this mood he sought cousin Celia and took her to supper. He examined her more critically now, finding her handsome, solid, and only passably interesting. He noted, too, that her manner lacked sprightliness and enthusiasm, and that the things she talked about didn't interest him in the least. He found himself apologising again and again for not having heard what she said. That was whenever there were questions for him to answer. He had, however, enough wit left to feel it was fortunate she did not ask questions more frequently. Meanwhile his eye wandered constantly towards a little table some distance off, which Miss Brooke and her American friend had all to themselves, the other two covers being as yet unappropriated. Once or twice he became aware that Celia's eye was following his. He saw a gleam of understanding flash across her face, followed by a flush whose meaning was obvious. But somehow he felt reckless.

An hour later he was with Miss Brooke again. At her laughing suggestion they had found a hiding-place, more "towards the upper regions," in order to keep out of the way of the man whose name had been written over, and who, indeed, never appeared. Miss Brooke was admiring an exquisite little painting of a picturesque boy looking over a rude wooden bridge on to a small stream. The work, which hung just opposite them, bore a well-known French signature, and had attracted her attention at once. The enthusiasm with which she spoke of the artist led Paul to inquire if she herself painted.

"I try to," she answered self-deprecatingly. "I am appallingly interested in my work. I always lose myself when talking about it."

She was evidently serious, and Paul was glad to have struck such a mood, which promised possibilities of intimate conversation.

"You have taken up art seriously?" he asked.

"One must do something to fill one's life," she replied, with unmistakable earnestness; and set Paul musing about the inability of fortune to compensate for a want of purpose in life, as he had, indeed, felt long ago. That a woman, however, should give expression to the sentiment surprised him. Her next words astonished him still more.

"I have always been ambitious, and I

might have achieved something in art if I hadn't wasted so many years trying other things."

"But, surely you must find the knowledge you have acquired worth having."

"I would willingly exchange it all for two years' progress in my work. The mistakes began by poppa discovering I was a musical genius, and as I was just mad to do something big in the world, I believed him. The next discovery was mine—that I was a great writer, and when, two years after that, an artist friend declared some sketches of mine were full of inspiration, my enthusiasm for writing fizzed out immediately, and I rushed into painting, and over to Paris to study. Of course, I'm only in the student stage, but my professor has given me distinct encouragement. In my heart I really believe I should succeed if only——" She broke off with a curious laugh, but went on almost immediately: "If only I don't transfer my enthusiasm to sculpture before long. You see I know my little ways. Besides, the temptation to change is as strong as it possibly can be. It would be such a distinction to have completed the round of the arts."

"Poetry would still be left untouched."

"Oh, I've written poetry as well. That was part and parcel of my literary mania."

"And naturally expired with it."

"No. Let me confess. Poetry is the one thing I keep up in order to be able to feel I am made of fine stuff. It's the one unsaleable thing I devote my time to, and without it I should feel utterly ignoble. With all my ambition to achieve greatness, I am quite unable to say how much of my enthusiasm is due to the hope of accompanying dollars."

Paul was startled for a moment, then laughed in high amusement at the idea of a railway king's daughter eking out her income by Art.

"I mean it. I'm not as noble as I look, but thank you for the compliment all the same. If I have allowed myself any illusions on the point, they were all dissipated when I heard of the price a Salon picture sold for last year. My feeling of envy was too naked to be mistaken—naked and unashamed. I don't know if you've ever experienced the sort of thing—whether you've ever written poetry to keep your self-respect."

"I fear writing poetry would be no test for me. I don't mean to imply that the result would *not* be unsaleable," he added, smiling, "but that I am not so avaricious as you profess to be. I am quite satisfied that my work in life shall bring me no return."

"I wish I were as fine as that," said Miss Brooke.

"I am afraid I am far from being fine,"

said Paul, modestly. "I am simply content with my fortune. As you said before, one must do something to fill one's life. I am only too grateful for the prospect of being able to employ my energies. So you see I am really selfish at bottom."

"We each appear to have a due sense of the clay in us, so let us agree we are neither of us precisely the saints we appear. But you've not yet told me in what particular way you purpose satisfying that selfishness of yours."

"Thereby hangs a long tale," said Paul, laughing again. "It is connected with the family tradition I mentioned to you before."

"I remember. Your father laid some injunction on you about converting missionary energies and subscriptions for home use."

"That is a quaint way of putting it. It is true his injunction first set me thinking, and it led to my developing certain Utopian ideas of my own. As the result, I am now studying architecture. No doubt you will think it a strange choice. There begins another dance, and we've both partners."

"How vexatious!" said Miss Brooke. "Just when I am so interested. I am really longing to hear all about your Utopia."

"I should so much have liked to tell you," murmured Paul, thinking he might even have sat out another dance if it were not for his foolish exclamation.

"Oh, but you're going to call, Mr. Middleton."

"I shall be very happy," said Paul, repressing a start.

She wrote her address for him on the back of his programme, adding, "I shall be in on Wednesday afternoon."

He thanked her and took her down to the dancing-room where she was pounced upon immediately, and he then discovered, to his surprise, that he and Miss Brooke *had* sat out two dances! Moreover, the frown which Celia gave him over her partner's shoulder as she waltzed by made him refer to his programme, when he found he had overlooked the little tick at the side of dance number fourteen.

CHAPTER II.

"A DAY and a half to wait before seeing Miss Brooke again," was Paul's first reflection the next morning. "All I should have laughed at as absurd a month ago, proves to be true. I am fast in the toils." And all through the day Miss Brooke filled his thoughts. He was, somehow, a different person from before, as if he had awakened from some sluggish torpor.

All his life Paul had suffered from an excess of parental love, which had considerably curtailed his freedom; and even when the death of his father a year before had left him his own master, he had no thought of living away from his mother, much to her secret gratification. Her fondness for him had been such that she had had him educated at home for several years, and was only persuaded to let him go to school under great pressure from her husband. She had established her influence over her boy from the beginning, and his pliable and obedient disposition had enabled her to maintain it now that he was grown up. His father, who had divided his time between collecting beautiful beetles, representing a rural constituency, enacting the good Samaritan, and, as Paul had told Miss Brooke, thundering and writing letters to the press against foreign missions, had cherished an ambitious career for his son. He himself, he felt, was a mere pawn on the parliamentary chessboard, and he dreamt of a really great political future for Paul, who, moreover, he hoped, would leave his mark on the social life of the generation by promoting the increase of public fine-art collections. Beautiful centres of art—beautiful buildings with beautiful contents—could be established, he argued, if the money subscribed for foreign missions could be used for the purpose; and he had the necessary statistics ready to hurl at the head of the sceptic.

Acting on the advice of a friend who considered the Bar afforded the best training in oratory, he began by placing the boy in a solicitor's office immediately after he had left college. Some eighteen months later the father was carried off in an epidemic of influenza. Paul, who had long since discovered that oratory *via* the law was not adapted to one of his temperament, had decision enough to desist from it. His attitude towards his sire's dream had never been a very reverent one, for he knew well he was not of the stuff of which Parliamentary leaders are made. But, as the affection between the two had been really strong, the son wished to respect the father's ideas so far as possible, if only for sentimental reasons; and, finding in himself a natural taste for making beautiful designs as well as an innocent love for illuminated books, old carvings and mouldings, and such curious antiques as had a real art value, it occurred to him he might make a thorough study of architecture from the art as well as the practical side. Later on he would design art galleries for the people, and set a movement on foot to promote their construction. Without taking himself too solemnly, he liked to think that what he purposed would have given his father pleasure; and he was always able to take good-humouredly such jesting remarks as had reference to his schemes.

Meanwhile mother and son had settled down in a small house in Elm Park Road. The country house was let on a long lease, as Mrs. Middleton did not wish to have the trouble of keeping it up, preferring to travel for three months in the year. The household consumed but a small part of their revenues, and consequently the amount of money in the family threatened to increase from year to year, despite that Mr. Middleton's good works were continued, and that Paul, going a-slumming, started additional good works on his own account.

Mrs. Middleton was only too pleased at Paul's leaving "that nasty dark, close office," asserting it must have injured his health. Besides, her faith in his talents was so absolute that she was certain he would one day be a very great man indeed, whatever the profession he espoused. So she ceded to him for his study perhaps the pleasantest room in the house. It was at the back and opened on to a narrow garden, so that he could saunter out occasionally and pace up and down. As he was here quite isolated, he never felt the need of having rooms elsewhere.

Despite the vigilance under which Paul

had grown up, he had yet managed to have one or two boyish love-affairs without his parents suspecting anything; and he had at times dreamt of an ideal love and an ideal happiness. But of late he had developed different notions, and had come to pride himself on his freedom from all mawkish sentiment. Notwithstanding this, he was chivalrous enough to believe that women were angels; which belief, curiously enough, was unimpaired by the fact that, in practice, he was a little bit afraid and suspicious of them. Nor did he always find them interesting; he would sooner play a game of chess any day than talk to one of them.

Cousin Celia was often at the house to join him and his mother at their quiet tea, and one day the idea entered his head that Mrs. Middleton had a certain pet scheme. But modesty prevented it from taking root in him, and he preferred to believe that the notion of a marriage between him and Celia had occurred only to himself, and would greatly surprise everybody else if he broached it. Celia was an orphan, and he had heard her pitied all his life. She was considered to possess an extraordinary share of good looks and an uncommon degree of affability. Good judges assured one another she would make an excellent wife, and Mrs. Middleton had taken good care that the said judges should discuss the girl in the presence of her boy, who could scarcely contend against so subtle an undermining. Despite his vague knowledge of the wiles of match-making, he began to persuade himself that he really liked Celia, and he played more and more with the idea of marrying her. The leading-strings were handled so lightly and skilfully, he would have been much astonished to hear that his inclinations were not absolutely uninfluenced. In Celia was all that straightforwardness by which he set such store; from her was absent all that caprice and flirtatiousness he was so afraid of. It was easy to know her wishes, easy to please her; and she had never made him the victim of moods.

And the more he thought of marrying her, the more he began to decry romantic love to himself. Whether it really existed or not he would not pretend to say, though, in the light of his own experience, he could just imagine its existence. Those old boyish ideas of his were all a mistake. And thereupon he fell back eagerly on the theory of sensible companionship as the only sound basis for marriage—which theory had now abruptly to be rejected.

Already Paul, promenading his garden whilst beautiful coloured plates of Egyptian decoration lay neglected on his table, was bothering himself as to whether he could leave Celia out of the account with a clear conscience. The question he kept asking himself was whether such attention as he had paid her could reasonably be interpreted as bearing any real significance. He was certain he had never actively made love to her, as he had always hesitated to begin, but he had seen a great deal of her of late and their intimacy had made great strides. Moreover, she had allowed him his five dances the evening before without a word of demur. He knew, too, he had often felt himself flushing on hearing her praised, feeling a sort of proprietary pride in the subject of discussion; and he wondered now if his demeanour on such occasions had been observed.

All these considerations caused him considerable uneasiness in view of the fact that he was perfectly sure now he did not want to marry her. Miss Brooke had come into his horizon, and lo! the whole world was changed. Oh, to be free to woo and win such a girl!

Suddenly he had a flash of shrewder insight, and he was able to find comfort in that first suspicion, which now returned to him, that his mother was really responsible for this Celia affair. Why—and his awakened mind now ran over a score of memories—he had scarcely ever met Celia out without his mother having supplied the impulse for his going to the particular place! He had been a fool not to see how she had worked matters from the beginning. And now there arose in him a shade of resentment against her, and his man's independence revolted for the first time against this subtle subordination of his will to hers. He had a definite perception—attended with a distinct sense of shame—of the fact that he had never really ceased to be, so far as she was concerned, the good little boy who had learnt his letters at her knee. He had an individuality of his own, he told himself, and it behoved him to play the part of a man. He should begin his emancipation at once by putting a prompt stop to "this Celia business."

CHAPTER III.

As Paul rang at the address Miss Brooke had scribbled down on his programme, his dominating thought was that American millionaire's daughters chose rather shabby houses to stay in. Though the name of the street had surprised him when he had first read it, he had yet conceived it possible she might be staying at some kind of private hotel; but he had not anticipated a dusty card with the word "apartments." He took it for granted her mother was with her, and, though he had not formed any clear conception of Mrs. Brooke, she looming mistily in his mind as a handsome, stately personage that had decidedly to be taken into the reckoning, he had wondered how she would receive him.

A maid-servant ushered him up two flights of stairs into a front room and announced his name. As he entered he was conscious of three persons sitting at the far end where a bright fire burned, and was somewhat startled to recognise the long lithe figure, the dark face and hair, and the piercing black eyes of the American Miss Brooke had danced with. A peculiar shade of expression flitted across the man's face, telling Paul the recognition was mutual. At the same time Paul was assuming that the bonneted and cloaked mature-looking lady was no other than Mrs. Brooke herself, and he wondered why she should receive callers when so obviously dressed for going out. Miss Brooke rose to greet him with a pleasant smile of welcome. In a simple dress with wide sleeves that fitted tight round the wrists, her short front hair, evenly divided, falling over her temples in rippling masses, she seemed less phantasmal and fairylike, less remote from this world—a being more humanly sweet and that one might dare to woo.

But unfortunately in that moment he became aware of the huge bulk of a high bed against the wall on his right, and a tall screen that cut off a corner of the room struck him as having the air of concealing something. Though he kept control over himself physically, his mind grew perfectly vacant. He did not dare to think —it seemed vain to make any surmise— but bowed to the bonneted lady as he heard Miss Brooke say: "Katharine, let me introduce my friend, Mr. Middleton— Mrs. Potter."

Paul had seldom felt so many emotions at one time. Added to his surprise at the expected Mrs. Brooke changing at the last moment into a Mrs. Potter, and to his bewilderment at being received in a bedroom, was a thrill of pleasure at Miss Brooke's reference to him as "my friend." He had, too, a sense of gratified curiosity at learning the next moment that the man's name was Pemberton; it was convenient, moreover, to have a definite symbol by which to refer to him in thought.

"I think the water's boiling, dear," said Mrs. Potter. "Doesn't it mean 'boiling' when steam comes out of the spout like that?"

"Not yet, Katharine. Half a minute more. You are just in nice time, Mr. Middleton, to get your cup of tea at its best." And Miss Brooke busied herself cutting up a big lemon into thin slices at a little table that was laid with a pretty Japanese tea-set.

"Lisa's tea is quite wonderful," chimed in Mrs. Potter. "I always spoil mine—I can never quite tell when the water boils. That's my pet stupidity."

For a moment Paul watched the artistic copper kettle as it sang its pleasant song. Mrs. Potter already struck him as an obviously cheerful personality, and he felt absurdly grateful to her for mentioning Miss Brooke's first name. He had not yet given up Mrs. Brooke, expecting her to enter the room very soon now; and he found it hard not to fix his gaze noticeably on the bed, half-surprised that everybody else ignored it, seeming totally unconscious that any such piece of furniture was there at all.

Mr. Pemberton took little part in the somewhat banal but good-humoured conversation that now sprang up, but drummed idly with his fingers on the settee on which he was lounging. Now and again a monosyllabic drawl fell languidly from him, and Paul read into this demeanour annoyance at his presence.

Mrs. Potter, he soon learnt—for the lady was loquacious—was a widow and a journalist on a three months' stay in Europe, of which she was passing a month in London, endeavouring to make as much copy out of it as possible. She related with glee, and without any apparent qualms of conscience, how she had "fixed up" accounts of various great society functions, writing her copy in the first person.

"Lisa is so good and helpful to me. I impose on her dreadfully. I should never havè been able to get them fixed up without her. And then her spelling is so perfect—she runs over my copy and puts it right in a jiffy."

"Lemon or cream, Mr. Middleton, please?" asked Miss Brooke. "Two lumps of sugar or one? What, none at all! Oh, yes, everybody thinks these cups sweetly pretty. I'm taking them home with me as a souvenir."

"What shall I do without you in Paris?" broke in Mrs. Potter again. "I shall be lost there. Can't I coax you to come back with me, Lisa dear?"

"Can't disappoint poppa," said Miss Brooke laconically.

"You'll have me to come to," drawled Mr. Pemberton.

"You'll be handy for some things, but your spelling's worse than mine," said Mrs. Potter; and somewhat irrelevantly went on to suppose that Paul must know Paris well.

Paul, alas! had only two visits to boast of, one of a week's, the other of two weeks' duration, both in the company of his mother. Whereupon a sound, as of a suppressed snigger, came from the direction of Pemberton.

Something like the truth had begun to dawn on Paul's mind, and he knew better now than to continue to expect Mrs. Brooke to appear. He had sufficiently gathered from the conversation that Miss Brooke was on her way home from Paris to America, and that she was going to travel alone, and had taken London *en route*, probably armed with letters of introduction. Most likely, he argued, she must have considered the one room sufficient for her needs, and had not anticipated callers. Or perhaps Americans, for all he knew, did not mind receiving callers in a bedroom. This, he concluded, was probably the case, as no one seemed in the least *gêné*, despite that the bed was such a palpable fact, and stood there in massive unblushingness. Otherwise an atmosphere of feminine daintiness seemed to surround Miss Brooke, transforming even this lodging-house bedroom.

However, he did not grasp the facts without an almost overwhelming sense of pain.

His romance had been rudely shattered at one blast, and he felt his breath draw heavily when he first comprehended Miss Brooke was on the point of leaving London. A sense of helplessness came upon him as he realised he could do nothing but just get through with his call. There seemed not the slightest chance now of his telling her about the career he purposed for himself. He had dreamed, too, of her showing him her verses, perhaps some of her sketches. But the presence of the others stood in the way. He would have liked to hate them both, but being forced to like Mrs. Potter, he had to bestow a double amount of dislike on Mr. Pemberton, which he was very glad to do. And then he wanted to know the exact relation between Mr. Pemberton and Miss Brooke. From a hint the "fellow" had dropped, it was clear he lived in Paris—where Miss Brooke had been living. Was he a relative? Who was he? Why was he in London? How came he to be at Mrs. Saxon's dance? For a moment Paul thought of asking Mrs. Saxon about him, and also about Miss Brooke, but he put the idea from him as underhand and unworthy.

Meanwhile the conversation went on, pleasant and banal. Mrs. Potter deluged Paul with questions about the London season and English painters and the Academy. She narrated the comicalities of her shopping expeditions, various little misadventures that had arisen from the different usage of everyday words by the two nations. By imperceptible stages along a tortuous and varied route they drifted on to the subject of love, and Mrs. Potter, still keeping the talk almost all to herself, related several touching romances of her friends' lives. Once or twice Paul's gloom was lightened by the smile of Miss Brooke that met his look each time he turned his face towards her. A lien, invisible to the others, seemed to be established between them.

At length Mrs. Potter, drawing Mr. Pemberton's attention to the hour, rose to go, and the two left together. Despite some mad idea of declaring himself to Miss Brooke there and then, which had occurred to him, Paul had also risen, but to his astonishment Miss Brooke drew her chair closer to the fire, and motioned him to take a seat in the opposite chimney corner. He obeyed as if hypnotised. "What would my mother think of this?" he asked himself, and awaited developments. As for Miss Brooke, at no moment did she seem aware of the slightest unconventionality in the situation.

"Katharine is so sweet," she began thoughtfully. "You can't imagine how pleased I was when she wrote she was coming. Charlie is piloting her about a little. He is so good-natured."

"Charlie is, I presume, Mr. Pemberton."

"Why, of course. And he'll be of so much use to her in Paris. He has a studio there. But I hope she won't fall in love with him," she added laughingly. "Katharine is so romantic; she is always in love with some man or other."

Though he knew as a general biological fact that women fall in love with men, Paul, despite all the love-stories he had read, had never yet been able to grasp it and admit it to himself as a fact of actual life. Somehow, he had always felt that the onus of falling in love and of courtship rested on men, and that it was very good and condescending of women to allow themselves to be loved at all. But Miss Brooke's way of talking seemed to take it for granted that it was a perfectly natural and proper thing for a woman to be in love, that romance was a thing a woman might own to without any shame; making him realise more distinctly than ever before that women were not so entirely passive and passionless. But all this he rather felt than thought, and it did not interfere with the sentence that was on the tip of his tongue; the outcome of his sense of disappointment and desolation at her threatened departure out of his life, which was only mitigated by the reflection that Pemberton was being left behind.

"And now you are going home!"

The words were obviously equivalent to a sigh of regret.

"But not for good, I hope," said Miss Brooke; and Paul's universe changed at once into a wonderful enchanted garden. "Of course, it will be very nice to be at home with poppa and mamma again, but I should not be leaving Paris from choice. I was making such progress at school that my professor was quite angry I couldn't stay. But perhaps I shall be back in a year's time. I certainly shall if everything goes well."

"I do hope it's nothing serious that calls you away, and that keeps you from your studies so long a time," exclaimed Paul fervently.

"From my point of view it's certainly serious," smiled Miss Brooke, good-humouredly. "As I've already tried to make you believe, I am a very greedy person, with a fondness for dollars, and the whole trouble is that they keep out of reach. Poor hard-worked poppa can't send me any more money just now, but he'll be getting a bigger salary next year, and I shall be able to go back and paint a masterpiece for the Salon. In the meanwhile I shall have to amuse myself as best I can sketching about the place, and watching poppa getting through big batches of couples. He's a minister—you know the cloth's hereditary in our family—and marries off people wholesale."

Till that moment Miss Brooke had been the railway king's daughter. For Paul to find now that she was a comparatively poor girl, whose anxiety to earn money by making her mark in art was no mere jesting pretence, involved a complete readjustment of his mental focus. But its instantaneity made the operation a violent one, especially as he strove hard not to exhibit any external signs of discomposure. At the same time a good deal that had bewildered him was explained, though there were points yet on which he needed enlightenment. And with all his astonishment went an unbounded admiration for the cheerful way in which she accepted her position, the lover's keen lookout for every scrap of virtue in the beloved seizing on this greedily for commendation. What a splendid, plucky girl she was! The glamour of his romance was heightened. Mere millionaires and all that appertained to them seemed suddenly prosaic.

Into what a bizarre misconception had he fallen! She herself was not to blame. If his mind had not been clogged up by what Thorn had told him beforehand he would not so persistently have misunderstood her references to money; but how should he have thought of challenging what he knew only now to have been a mere speculative rumour? There had been nothing in her appearance and personality to belie that rumour, and, as obviously she was not called upon to contradict statements about herself she had never heard, such manifestations of the truth as had since become visible to him had only served to mystify him.

The way, too, she had taken certain things for granted as perfectly natural and proper, somewhat astonished him, to wit, her inviting him to call here, her reception of him in a bedroom, and his presence alone with her now. These facts contravened the ideas in which he had been brought up, and he could only suppose that American ideas probably differed from English. This surmise seemed, on the whole, corroborated by the glimpse he had had that day into the spirit of the American independent woman—a type entirely new to him—as exemplified both by Mrs. Potter and Miss Brooke.

He asked how soon she was leaving, and learnt she was sailing on the Saturday, so that barely two days of London remained to her. He did not like the idea at all, as he had formed the hope he might somehow see her again before her departure.

"My berth is taken," explained Miss Brooke, perhaps amused by his evident discontent. "Some boxes have gone on. Besides, I could not stay here any longer. Dollars are getting scarce. I'm going to have some more tea—won't you join me?"

"Willingly." He wanted to stay longer, and tea, by filling the time plausibly, would help to lessen his constraint at the original position in which he found himself.

"I am so pleased you were able to call!" went on Miss Brooke, as she poured out the beverage. "You haven't forgotten your promise to tell me all about your work—and your Utopia as well," she added, smiling, and handing him his cup.

Her sweetness as she spoke enchanted him. When he himself had been hesitating on the brink of the chasm, with what ease had she taken him across it at one leap! Soon he found himself telling her how he had come to abandon his father's ideas and plan out his life his own way, with as much emotion as if he were relating his inmost secrets to an affianced wife. And certainly no affianced wife could have listened with a graver attention, or more sympathetic demeanour.

"Has it ever occurred to you to study architecture at Paris?" she asked. "The

Beaux Art School is, I think, one of the finest in the world, and you could scarcely get a more artistic atmosphere."

The effect of her remark was as that of an electric spark that fuses many elements into one new whole. He was conscious of a struggling chaotic mass of thought, followed by a clear perception of the conditions of his existence in all its bearings. And in a flash he had made up his mind to plunge into the delicious indefiniteness of what offered itself. A soft purple haze floated before him as in a dream, and an odour of incense and a harmony of sweet sounds seemed to steal upon him. And the haze, parting a moment, allowed him a glimpse of a magic city in its depths. And in that city, he knew, were "Lisa" and himself.

That was to be the future! The awakening of the man in him was complete. By an abrupt mastercoup he would wrench himself away from the influences that had well-nigh reduced him to a puppet. His reply to Miss Brooke now would be the beginning of the necessary forward impulse.

"The idea has not come to me, though, of course, I should have had to consider the question of a formal course before very long. But I like the suggestion very much."

"Lots of the boys take the course there," added Miss Brooke. "There are, of course, many more American than English boys, but you'll find them all a sociable set."

He asked for details about the student life, and Miss Brooke tried to give him some notion of it. In this way quite half an hour slipped by, during which Paul became worked up to a high pitch of enthusiasm and took care to leave no doubt in Miss Brooke's mind that his decision was finally taken.

"Charlie, too, might be useful to you," said Miss Brooke, as Paul rose to take his leave. "I'm sure he'd be delighted to be of service to you. And how nice, too, if we were to meet there again! Perhaps we shall."

Her face gleamed as with the pleasure of anticipation.

"I shall always bear the hope with me," said Paul gravely; and, wishing her a pleasant crossing, he bade her "good-bye."

"Let us say '*Au revoir*' rather," and once again she pressed his hand, which was more than he had dared hope for.

But what had "Charlie" to do with Miss Brooke? he asked himself a thousand times that evening.

CHAPTER IV.

A MONTH later—about the beginning of June—Paul had entered the École des Beaux Arts as a student of architecture. Not to have succeeded in tearing himself away would have been to lose all self-respect. He had determined to justify himself to himself, to prove he had a will he need not be ashamed of. Thus it was that his astonished mother and a favourite uncle—Celia's guardian—who both had a good deal to say about Paris and its temptations, expended their speech to no purpose.

Paul entered into his student life with zest, working hard and conscientiously in a very methodical fashion. He allowed himself, however, plenty of time for enjoying the city; going to the theatres, and peeping into all the show places, and hunting up curios at old shops, and lounging and playing billiards at the cafés, and drinking beer *al fresco* on the boulevards. Occasionally he rode in the Bois, or made excursions up and down the Seine, and into the neighbouring country—mostly, of course, in company, for he soon struck acquaintance with some of the men, many of whom he found had to manage on very little money. So he said nothing about his own easy circumstances, rather enjoying the two-franc seat at the theatre and the fifteen-centime ride on the tops of tramcars. When he wanted expensive amusement he went alone.

No one he knew had so far mentioned Miss Brooke's name, and though he was often on the point of asking one or other of his new friends about her, some instinct invariably restrained him. He had nurtured his love for her, all his solitary thought turning to her, and it seemed a sort of sacrilege to make even the most innocent inquiry about her in her absence. This waiting for her in silence was part of the romance.

He understood the American girl a little better now, fellow-students having introduced him to girl friends—that is to say, he was better acquainted with her and her ways. And he was satisfied that whatever appeared right to Miss Brooke, no matter how much it violated his own notions, must be right absolutely. With her the fact of riches or poverty was reduced to a mere indifferent background, against which her personality stood out in all its charm and dignity. A girl like her could make her home in one room, and yet make you welcome in it with as much ease and grace as any lady in a fine drawing-room.

Time passed, and still nobody, by any chance, referred to Miss Brooke. This was not surprising, for Paris was large, and American girl students were plentiful and scattered all over it. Moreover, a girl who had gone home months before was likely to be soon forgotten. Pemberton he had never met, but he had seen him just once from the top of a tramcar. The hot weather came on and Paul passed a delicious month at Montmorency in company with one of the men. After his return he settled to work again, and the months went by almost without his keeping count of them—for, Miss Brooke having mentioned a year as the time she was likely to remain in America, he would not look for her till the spring came on again. In the meanwhile he inflicted much misery on himself by speculating as to whether home and home ties might not have absorbed for good so ideal and affectionate a girl as he conceived her to be, especially after so long a residence abroad. But deep down was implanted in him an unswerving faith in her coming, and, though the manner of their meeting had been left so undefined, he was certain there would be no difficulty when the time came, and that his life after that would be one long fairy tale.

The spring came at last, and with it *vernissage* at the Salon. Paul knew one or two men who were exhibiting, so he decided to pass his afternoon at the Palais de l'Industrie. The tens of thousands that thronged the galleries made picture-inspection difficult and tedious; but the crowd itself presented many compensating features of interest. Paul was hoping, too, he might see Miss Brooke there, as it was not impossible she might by now be back in Paris. Occasionally he fancied a girl resembled Miss Brooke, but when, after infinite striving, he had got close to his quarry, he found the points of likeness were but few. Once or twice the fair one eluded his pursuit, and got irretrievably swallowed up.

On his going to *déjeuner* the next day, at a little restaurant close by the school, where he was in the habit of dropping in at mid-day—he dined in the evening in state at a more pretentious establishment—there sat Miss Brooke herself at a table at the end of the room, her face towards the door. None of the usual clients had yet arrived, as it was a trifle early, and *mademoiselle* was distributing the newly-written menus among the various tables. In any case he must have caught sight of her at once, as the cluster of sharp red and black wings that shot up from one side of the little toque, which just seemed to rest on her hair, drew the eye at once. Her face showed glowing and bright, set above the dark mass of her stuff dress. As the door swung to she looked up from the menu she had been studying.

"How do you do, Mr. Middleton? You seem real scared to see me."

Her greeting seemed as calm and laughing as if they had but parted the day before, and Paul felt some vague dissatisfaction with it—he did not quite know why. It seemed, somehow, as if there were no romance between them at all, as if they were the merest acquaintances. Perhaps it was that the pent-up emotion of months of waiting needed more dramatic expression than this commonplace situation afforded.

He asked permission, and sat down opposite her, scarcely knowing what to say to her first.

"Can you tell me whether *cervelle de veau* is anything good to eat? It's the only unfamiliar thing on the menu, and my only hope."

He took the sheet of paper as she held it to him, but found the dish was equally unknown to him. They appealed to *mademoiselle*, who informed them, "*C'est dans la tête.*"

"I wonder if she means 'brains.' I was hoping not to have to translate *cervelle* literally."

"I am not afraid of experimenting," suggested Paul.

"For my benefit. That is real kind of you. Whenever I've been curious about things with strange names, I've always had to order them, which is rather an expensive way of increasing one's French vocabulary."

When the dish came, neither Paul nor Miss Brooke liked the curly look of it, so they fell back on *bifteck*, salad, cheese, and fruit.

"And so you are here after all," said Miss Brooke, musingly.

"Why? Did you think I was not serious about coming?"

"I didn't mean that. My expression was a sort of acknowledgment to myself that I had found you—or rather, to be proper, that you had found me."

His heart fairly leaped with pleasure. She had certainly then thought of him during the past months!

"I must thank the happy chance that led you in here," he murmured, feeling his emotion at length control him.

"Happy chance!" She charmed his ear with a ripple of laughter. "Why, I've exhausted almost every restaurant near the

Beaux Arts, that being the most feminine way of pursuing you. The mathematical theory of probability—college learning *does* prove useful at times—told me the happening of the event, that is, of the event I wanted to happen, was a certainty. For some particular restaurant or other is a habit which everybody contracts; it is, indeed, the first vice one picks up in Paris. And it's a habit that can't be broken. Day after day you revolt—if you're a man, you swear— against the *cuisine*. Things are becoming intolerable. Time was when everything was perfect, when the menu was varied, and always included your favourite dishes; when one could eat the salad without too close an inspection of the under-side of the leaves, and when the wine at eighty centimes a litre didn't turn blue or taste like ink. To-day is, most certainly, the last time you will ever set foot in the place. But the morrow comes, and at *déjeuner* time your feet bear you there again, and you are so meek about it that you scarcely protest."

"That is just my experience," he confessed.

"I was sure it would be. That is what enabled me to calculate so infallibly. You see I speak my thoughts quite unashamed. Paris makes one so frightfully immodest."

"I'm glad, then, I didn't take it into my head to apply the same method in my search for you. Not only would it have upset your mathematics, but, having no particular landmark, I might have wandered on forever. All the same, I have kept my eyes open. In fact, I was hoping to see you yesterday at *vernissage*."

"Were you there?" she exclaimed. "What a silly question!" she added immediately, laughing. "What I meant to say was *I* was there. But, of course, it was quite impossible to find any one in such a crowd."

Paul noticed with pleasure that the conversation on both sides assumed the fact of a positive rendezvous between them. Miss Brooke went on to chatter about the *vernissage*.

"I see this morning's *Herald* puts us down as a low lot. Its reporter must be very *exigeant*. In spite of our presence he insists the models gave the *ton* to the assembly."

"Were there many models present?" asked Paul. "I don't remember seeing any."

"There were quite enough of them to be noticeable. Perhaps you thought they were all countesses."

"I did have some such idea," he admitted. "I didn't know models dressed like countesses."

"They do when their artists take them to *vernissage*. Which affords food for reflection."

Paul felt slightly embarrassed and did not answer.

"And now," resumed Miss Brooke, contemplating her *cœur à la crême*, "if I may venture to intrude on your reflections, will you please pass me the sugar?"

"Is it long since you returned?" he inquired soon. "I was going to ask you before, only the *cervelle* puzzle arose and somehow I forgot."

"Just three weeks," she replied. "Poppa had his bigger salary, and as it was getting tedious seeing couples married I made haste to come over again. You can't imagine how impatient I was to get back in time for *vernissage*. It gives such a fillip to your ambitions to see crowds round your friends' pictures, and to read about them in the papers; it makes you realise your own powers, and sets you wondering why *you* hadn't dared to send something in. When you are tired of lamenting your folly you begin to admire your modesty, and of course you remember that modesty is the mark of true genius."

"And you had all those thoughts?"

"Oh, no! They are the thoughts I should have had if I hadn't been busy admiring the dresses. The pictures must wait—I shall be going again to see those, perhaps two or three times. Most students do. One is supposed to learn from them, but in practice one only criticises. The boys say everything is rotten. We girls pretend to agree with them, only, of course, it wouldn't be proper to express our opinion as violently as that. Do you dine here as well?"

"I dine as the whim takes me. You see I haven't yet acquired a habit for evening wear. Not every Bohemian can make that boast."

Miss Brooke laughed. "Bohemians mostly acquire bad habits for evening wear. But I'm going to cut Bohemianism altogether so far as my meals are concerned, and settle down in a *pension.* Two or three of the girls live there, and they report well of it. I also made friends while crossing with a girl who was being consigned there."

He asked whether she had had a good crossing, and whether she were a good sailor. Miss Brooke replied that the weather had been perfect the whole way and she had enjoyed herself, and she proceeded to entertain him by relating incidents of the passage. Meanwhile the little restaurant had filled, and was nearly empty again. They rose at last and settled their *additions.* Paul then noticed that Miss Brooke had her painting materials with her, and insisted on carrying them so far as her school. They stepped out into the sunshine, and became aware how fine a day it was.

"The afternoon almost tempts me to cut the Beaux Arts," said Paul.

"By the way, how are you getting on there?" asked Miss Brooke.

He was only too eager to tell her of his progress, and to discuss his chances of a medal. He also gave her an account of the new friends he had made—he liked the American "boys" very much, was indebted to them for endless kindnesses.

"Why didn't you look up Charlie?" she asked suddenly.

"How could I?" he asked, annoyed at the mention of the man's name, reminding him, as it did, of the apparent and inexplicable intimacy between the two, and also telling him they must already have seen each other.

"You could easily have found him if you had inquired among the boys. He lives in his studio and he has scarcely left it the whole time I've been away. By the way, you remember Katharine, don't you? She's married again. To her editor this time. This is my school."

They came to a standstill and faced each other to say "good-bye."

"I scarcely feel like working this afternoon," observed Miss Brooke. "My laziness really overpowers my ambition. Did you not say something before, Mr. Middleton, about your being tempted to cut the Beaux Arts? Do be nice and yield to that temptation. I want to give way to mine so badly, but being a woman I daren't do anything unless somebody else is doing it at the same time."

Paul's fibres of resistance did not relax gradually; they collapsed all at once.

"Well," he laughed. "I've been so good all along, I think I've earned the right to play truant for once."

"Mr. Middleton! That's bringing morality into it again, and I wanted to indulge in undiluted wickedness. You have to carry my box as I'm sufficiently occupied in holding up my skirts. I'll give you some tea afterwards as a reward."

They strolled slowly in the sunshine, making for the river and crossing by the Pont des Arts; and passed through the Jardins des Tuileries, where the freshness of the greens, and the playing fountains, and the leafy trees, and the pretty children, and the odour of lilac proclaimed the spring. They sauntered across the Place de la Concorde and into the shady avenues of the Champs Elysées, where huge spots of sunlight freckled the ground; talking the while of the life of the city, of the foreign elements, of the Old and New Salons. Miss Brooke explained how her own day was spent. Seven o'clock in the morning found her punctually at school, and she worked two hours before taking her *café au lait*, afterwards continuing till midday. In the afternoon she usually copied and studied at the Louvre or Luxembourg. Such had been the routine of her work before, and she had had no difficulty in falling into it again. She could not hope to exhibit even next year, as she could neither afford a studio nor the expense of models. At the present she was living with some friends at their *appartement* in the Avenue de Wagram. After their departure at the end of May she would enter into the *pension*, which was within a stone's throw of her school.

Paul, eagerly listening to all these details, was only conscious in a far-off way of the eternal roll of smart carriages in the roadway, or of the multitude of children playing under the trees in charge of *bonnes*, whilst the mammas sat about on chairs, chatting, or with books or needlework. Onward the pair strolled past the Arc de Triomphe and down the great Avenue into the Bois de Boulogne, only stopping to rest by the laughing lake. Here the appeal of the water and the moored boats soon became irresistible. They fleeted the remainder of the afternoon ideally, till Miss Brooke announced it was time to repair to the Avenue de Wagram. Paul was afraid of her friends—he was scarcely presentable.

"Be calm, my friend," she reassured him. "We shall have a nice little tea all to ourselves. The others have gone to Versailles and are only coming back in time to dine. We dine *chez nous*, as we have a *bonne* who cooks. Of course I can't be in to *déjeuner*, as the distance is too great from my school. You must come one evening and I'll present you."

He thanked her for the suggestion, glad to welcome every arrangement that promised in any way to throw their lives together, for he had been not a little afraid he might not after all have the opportunity of seeing very much of her.

As Miss Brooke made the tea in the pretty drawing room of the cosy flat, Paul began to realise with surprise how much progress their friendship had made in that one day. His dream had turned out true! He was so happy that the consciousness of all but the moment faded from him. London, his mother, Celia, and even chess were for the time absolutely non-existent. "Charlie," too, was forgotten, as the obnoxious name had not again dropped from Miss Brooke's lips.

He took his leave at last, filled with joy by Miss Brooke's promise to run in on the morrow to *déjeuner* at the same little restaurant. But as he turned from the broad stairway into the hall, he almost collided in his pre-occupation with a tall well-dressed man. Both murmured "*Pardon!*" and pursued their ways. Paul had seen the other's face, but he had taken several steps forward before the features sank into his brain, and he realised with a great shock they were those of "Charlie."

CHAPTER V.

However, Miss Brooke said nothing to him about Charlie in the days that followed, though he saw her often. Without it being specially mentioned again, it was somehow understood they were, for the present, to meet at mid-day at the little restaurant, and, moreover, she allowed him to take her several times to the two Salons. He might easily have dragged in references to Pemberton, but he felt it would not be right to do so for the mere purpose of discovering what it would have been an impertinence to demand outright.

And the more his *camaraderie* with Miss Brooke became an established fact, the more did this question of Charlie disturb him. He had discovered by this time that a harmless friendship between a man and a girl was by no means unusual among the students and was not necessarily assumed to imply matrimonial intentions. He knew, moreover, that such friendships grew rapidly on this soil where the English-speaking students gravitated together during the years of their voluntary exile. But, if this thought pacified him as to Miss Brooke and Charlie, the very pacification carried with it a sting. For it led to the further tormenting suspicion that Miss Brooke did not take the relationship between her and himself as seriously as he would have liked her to. Her conduct and bearing towards him were all he could wish, yet he seemed to feel behind them a stern limit to the intimacy, a barrier, as it were, that might bear on its face: "I am put here by way of giving you a reminder you are not to make any mistakes as to the extent of your rights over this property."

Sometimes, indeed, in envisaging the position, he came to the conclusion that this was entirely due to his own imagination and that he might safely ask her to share his life. But at that point uncertainty would rise again, warning him that to make any such impulsive proposition just then might be to jeopardise the future of his romance. The remembrance of the distress caused him by his effort to determine the precise degree of Celia's claim on him by reason of his having engaged her for five dances in the same evening intruded in grotesque contrast now that he was endeavouring to determine the precise degree of his claim on Miss Brooke.

Despite these prickings, and despite Charlie, sweetness predominated in his life.

He felt untrammelled and unwatched over, recalling with a shudder the old strands that had tethered him. Though he wrote regularly to his mother, whom he had seen twice last autumn, on her way southward and on her return, all reference to Miss Brooke was excluded from his letters. He would not discuss his relation to her with anybody else, foreseeing that would only lead to a deal of useless and perhaps endless talk.

After Miss Brooke had moved to the *pension*, where she had arranged to take all her meals, he no longer saw her every day. But it was understood he could take his chance of finding her at home whenever he chose to call in the evenings. She generally received him in her little oblong sitting-room on the second floor, that opened out on a pleasant balcony, overlooking the street. He soon grew to love this room, to the decorations of which she had added a huge Japanese umbrella, which hung from the ceiling, and two Japanese lights, and a piece of Oriental tapestry, besides her personal nicknacks. Paul's usual lounging-place, whilst Miss Brooke gave him his after-dinner coffee, was an old cretonne-covered ottoman, on which a broken spring made a curious hump, and over his head were suspended some book-shelves. Now and again he would find other callers, of both sexes, for Miss Brooke was "at home" once a week to all her friends. Of course, Paul did not abuse his privilege, but firmly restricted the number of his visits. Occasionally, too, he had the happiness of taking her to dine at some one or other of the great cafés on the Grands Boulevards, and they would stroll back together along the river bank, enchanted by the wonderful nocturnes. On Sunday sometimes, they would make an excursion beyond the fortifications to some rural spot, she taking her paint-box and sketching lazily whilst they talked; and if, on rare afternoons, he left his work, and looked in at the Luxembourg to find her deftly plying her brush in her big blue coarse linen apron, with its capacious pockets, she seemed by no means displeased.

Every legitimate topic was talked over between them. He had long since exhausted the theme of his own life, that is, he had told it so far as he cared to tell it. Celia, for one thing, did not appear in it, and there were one or two little matters he was especially careful to suppress. He felt vaguely saint-like, when, in the course of this judicious selection from his biography, he arrived at his slumming experiences, and hinted at his charities, which were being continued during his absence. Miss Brooke repaid the confidence in kind, enabling him, by her various reminiscences, to reconstruct a fairly continuous account of her existence, which, it never struck him, might also be selected.

They drifted, too, into the realm of ideas, exchanging their notions on—among other things—love and platonic friendship. They discussed the last-mentioned phenomenon in great detail, Paul, aflame with self-consciousness, but quite unable to pierce beneath the sphinx-like demeanour with which Miss Brooke made her impartial and freezingly impersonal statements. From ideas they passed on to the consideration of conduct and how it should be determined under divers subtle conditions.

"Yes, but don't you really think that one *ought* to listen to such an appeal if. . . . ," she would gravely interpose with her sweet voice as her brush made sensuous strokes on the canvas. And Paul became more and more impressed with the nobility of her soul, and strove likewise—as was but natural in the circumstances—to impress her with the nobility of his. He usually felt ethically perfect after such conversations, and, had the occasion immediately arisen, it would have found him equal to acting along the lines of the "ought" laid down by Miss Brooke. He imagined that he certainly was receiving endless benefit from this threshing out of things with a quick and sympathetic personality.

So ran by a couple of months, "Charlie" continuing to be the chief cause of disturbance in Paul's existence. The two men had by now met several times at Miss Brooke's, had saluted civilly, but had little to say to each other. Paul felt sure his hatred was returned, and neither showed the least disposition to become better acquainted. Neither asked the other to dine or drink, or play billiards, or even to walk with him, and if rarely they passed in the street a nod was all they exchanged. The lines of their lives occasionally met in a point, but never ran together.

The enmity between them only became irksome when no others were present, but never did Miss Brooke herself manifest the least suspicion of it. Whatever the relation between Miss Brooke and Pemberton, it never seemed to interfere in practice with the relation between Miss Brooke and himself. She alluded to "Charlie" in her talk much more freely than heretofore, but always apropos, always impersonally, just as she might casually mention Katharine, who was so happy now. Charlie had such and such a habit, such and such a way of looking at things, such and such ideas of art.

But Paul's jealousy grew till he became well-nigh intolerable to himself. It made him resort to underhand watchings, from the mere thought of which, in saner moments, he shrank with shame and remorse. But he had thus ascertained that Charlie was, if anything, a more frequent visitor than himself, and had less scruples in the matter of standing on ceremony.

CHAPTER VI.

ONE night Paul was at the Opera when he caught sight of Miss Brooke and Pemberton with her. His evening was spoilt and he left at once. He felt both angry and hurt, for he had seen her for a few minutes in the afternoon, and she had said nothing about her plans for the evening beyond warning him it was highly probable she might not be at home.

The climax had come. He was determined that things should not continue as they were. If Miss Brooke simply regarded their connection as a mere students' companionship, agreeable to both parties but strictly temporary, then he must end it immediately. Miss

Brooke must at once be made aware of what this friendship meant to him. What he had so far deemed inexpedient seemed to him the only expediency—to stake all on one coup.

In the stress of the crisis the prejudices that were his by inheritance and teaching, and that his new life had caused to slumber, asserted themselves again, crying aloud against these friendships. Miss Brooke ought never to have expected him to be proof against that sort of thing, of which he had never had experience. Pemberton might be able and content to flutter round without hurt, but he himself had been a lost man from the beginning.

It soothed him to map out the future as he wished it to be, and all seemed so natural and reasonable that, if she cared for him in the least, she could not but admit his views on every point. He felt himself filled with an infinite longing, an infinite tenderness. He would surround her with his love so that escape from it should be impossible. It should permeate every fibre of her being, and she should in the end come to him and give up everything to fulfil the duties of a wife, presiding over his household, absorbing herself in his career, and giving all her thought to the unity their two lives would constitute. Of course, she could paint in such time as was left to her, and any glory she might achieve would redound to the credit of his name. Still when a woman had once become a wife, he argued, her ambition generally faded. Wifehood was absorbing. Greater glory than that of being a perfect wife there could not be.

A few days later, when his emotion had somewhat calmed down, and he could trust himself sufficiently to see her, he called at the *pension*, but, as had happened occasionally from the beginning, he did not find her at home. So the next morning he sent her a great heterogeneous mass of flowers with the half-jesting, half-reproachful hope they might meet with better fortune than he. Whereupon he immediately received a letter explaining she had passed the previous evening with some very nice people in the Avenue Kléber, and announcing her intention of taking him there on the morrow. Would he dine early and call for her? She thanked him for the flowers in a postscript, saying they had transformed her room into a veritable bower.

At the time appointed he climbed the well-known two flights of stairs and the *bonne* showed him into the little room, saying *mademoiselle* would join him "in a little minute." Several big minutes passed, and then the door-hanging was pushed aside and Miss Brooke stood smiling at him. She had always appealed to his æsthetic side, giving him the sense of contemplating an exquisite piece of art-work; but the particular impression he had to-night differed from all previous ones. Her figure seemed slenderer in its black net evening dress, covered with bead-work that glistened with a wonderful shading of green into blue and blue into green. Above the turquoise-blue velvet trimming of the bodice, her long neck made a dazzling whiteness, and her face looked pink and babyish, whilst her curls lay about with just a shade more severity than usual. She wore a necklace of turquoises set in antique gold, and in her hair was a big gold comb inset with the same stones, irregularly cut. The note of colour thus given made her blue eyes appear like two large jewels amid the constellation. Paul told himself he had never realised before *how* beautiful those eyes were. The lightly-parted lips intensified the babyishness, so that she ceased to be the independent, self-willed girl, fitting in rather with that other conception he had lingered on as the ideal she might develop into as his wife—a woman clinging to her husband and glad of his strength.

He was sure he saw her now as she really was. The conditions of her life were alone to blame for forcing on her the necessity of a career. Woman's true sphere was the home. An outside existence subjected to hardening influences a delicate soul whose very nature was to thirst for tender nurture and love. Such had always been his mother's conviction; such was his fervent belief. The association of Miss Brooke with money-earning seemed an ugly blot on the universe.

There seemed, too, a tenderer, more intimate quality in her voice, and a sort of clinging in her touch as she went down the stairway with her hand on his arm. That forbidding barrier of which he had always been conscious had vanished!

"It's the McCook's last 'At-Home,'" she explained, as the *voiture* began to move. "They are such nice people—I'm sure you'll like them. Dora's an old college chum of mine, and she's asked me to stay with her to-night. Dora and I chat such a deal when we get together, and we always enjoy sitting up nice and quiet by ourselves after everybody else has gone. I told her you would escort me home, but she seemed quite shocked at the idea. As if you haven't escorted me back from the theatre! Dora has become quite conventional since her marriage. She used to argue with her mother and do pretty well as she liked not so very long ago. Now I believe her mother shocks her sometimes. She's leaving with her husband in a few days for Perros-Guirec, and they're going to take me with them."

Her words rang with a childlike joy. He asked where Perros-Guirec was in a voice that was somewhat desolate at the prospect of losing her.

"It's in Brittany—a whole day's journey from Paris. I was there two years ago, and sketched most of the time. Everybody is thinking of leaving now, the heat will soon be getting unbearable. The Grand Prix has been run, the Battle of Flowers has been fought, and the Allée de Longchamps is deserted. All the smart people are in *villégiature*. How nice is the evening after the sultry day!"

They were passing through the Boulevard St. Germain. Miss Brooke was sitting just close enough to Paul for them to touch with the swaying of the carriage. He felt singularly happy. The hushed sounds of the city over which the dusk hung mystic came to him like a soft sustained tone of music; its lights gleamed in upon them with magic rays. He was conscious of the great dark masses of palaces, of shadowy pedestrians moving noiselessly on the side-paths. No fever in the air now, only a far-reaching calm.

"The night makes one almost sorry to leave Paris," resumed Miss Brooke. Her voice made the harmonies sweeter, blending them all into one perfect harmony.

"But the breezes, and the woods, and the rye-fields, and the farm-houses with their delicious old oak presses, and the kind-hearted people, and the quaint children who love to watch you sketch and see you squeeze the paint out of the tubes—the memory of all these things draws you back to them. I long for Brittany almost as much as I once longed to leave everything and everybody and be just myself—and by myself. It seems so long ago now."

She had almost unconsciously moved closer to him now.

"Won't you tell me when that was—Lisa?"

It was the first time he had dared to call her by this name. In his longing to utter it in articulate speech it had rushed to the tip of his tongue.

"It was three years ago—before I came here. Every place had associations that hurt me. I wanted to get away—to work, work, work. I seemed to hate everybody. So I came here, and for months I thought I was as hard as a stone. Then one day I found myself angry with a girl—a fellow-student—and I was quite surprised to find I could feel at all. And then I was suddenly glad I was a human being again."

Her voice melted away into the vast murmur of the soft-twinkling city. Beyond the fact that he was selfishly glad she had had trouble—it afforded him the exquisite pleasure of sympathy—there was no active thought in him now, no estimation of the position. His soul alone dominated; it had been moved to responsiveness and it now wrought out its mood, subtly surrounding her, he felt, with its comfort.

They crossed the mysterious, glistening river, and came upon the myriad flame-points of the Place de la Concorde. They turned into the Champs Elysées betwixt woods enchanted by the sorcerer Night; catching glimpses of palaces of light amid the trees whence melody came floating, mingled with the incense of the summer.

"Won't you tell me, Lisa—that is, if you think you can trust me."

It was sweet to exercise the privilege of calling her "Lisa." He felt it was his for always now.

"I know I can trust you, Paul. Would you really care to hear? Of course you would," she continued quickly, giving him no time to reply. "What a silly question for me to ask! Still there is little to tell!

I loved a man. We were to be married. His mind was poisoned against me by an enemy. He was harsh and unjust. A few words sum all up. He is married to another. A commonplace chapter, is it not? But to have lived through it—to have lived through it!"

He grew dazed and white. "To have lived through it!" Those simple words seemed to his comprehending mood athrob with the sobbing of great grief.

"But you do not love him now?" he breathed.

"No, no! All is over now. But I brooded and brooded and thought—the experience made me a woman. Life is a serious thing to me now. I feel better and stronger for what I have suffered. But the memory remains."

"You have nothing to reproach yourself with, Lisa. Surely there are happier memories in store for you. It is for you but to shape the future."

He longed for her impulsive "How?" and had his answer ready. It seemed a strange thing, but this confession of a past love, this telling of a great sorrow in her life, had wrought a spell upon him. His eyes were full of tears. In that moment his love for her seemed to have increased a thousandfold. The surprise with which the revelation had overwhelmed him was lost in the rush of pity. She had suffered, and by his love he would make everything up to her.

But now there came a sudden change, slight in its outward manifestation, but felt by him like a chill blast, for his soul vibrated to hers, registering every subtle shade of her mood. She did not speak immediately, and he knew that moment of silence was fatal.

They had passed the round point of the Champs Elysées, and the woods and gardens had ended. Only the giant *hôtels* rose on either hand. There seemed more carriages darting about now, a greater movement of life, a general sense of disenchantment in the air, of an awakening from a dream to the clattering reality of things. Paul realised that the spell was broken.

Miss Brooke had turned her head for a moment to look through the window.

"We shall be there in two or three minutes now," she said, as a sort of natural outcome of her ascertaining their exact whereabouts. "I am afraid I must rather have depressed you. It is scarcely courteous to our hostess for us to arrive in so gloomy a mood."

She gave a little laugh which set his every nerve a-tingle, so certainly did its ring lack the appealing quality that had brought him so close to her. It seemed to thrust him back abruptly and brutally.

"Tell me, Paul, haven't you ever had any love affairs?" she went on to ask, and there was a suspicion of banter in her tone. "I've told you all about my tragedy, now tell me about yours or all yours. I know we've told each other all our lives before, but of course we both bowdlerized. The most interesting parts have yet to be told."

As she had asked him a direct question he felt constrained to answer it. He found himself considering whether his relation to Celia need count as a love affair, but he was so convinced he had never been in love with her at all that he decided he could leave her out without doing violence to his conscience. Altogether there had been in his life two very minor and foolish amourettes that might have became entanglements; one with a barmaid when he was in the lawyer's office, some of the clerks having persuaded him the girl "was gone on him," the other with a simple maiden of sixteen, the daughter of a market gardener, which idyll had proceeded at his father's country seat. Paul told the latter—it was a boyish passion that had come to nothing and stood for nothing in his life; the former he was ashamed of. "I proposed to her and gave her a mortal fright. She was so scared she ran away. We were both shamefaced when we met again, and my spurt of pluck was at an end. I dared not say another word to her, and somehow we drifted out of being sweethearts. I was barely nineteen at the time."

Miss Brooke laughed again heartily, but Paul only felt the gloomier.

"Tell me some more, please. You put

me into quite a cheerful humour. What was your next love affair?"

She had resumed her old militant badinage.

"There is nothing more in my biography that is likely to entertain you," he answered evasively.

"Is it so bad as that, Paul? I think you might tell me all the same. I'm not easily shocked."

"You mistake me. I have told you all," he replied, driven to the lie direct.

"Come, come, Mr. Paul. In a woman one might expect such a want of candour. But suppose I tell you *my* other affairs—will that encourage you to tell me yours? Is it a bargain?"

"Your other affairs?" he repeated.

"Did you imagine I've had only one in my life? That's paying me a very poor compliment. This is our destination."

"Why do you tease me, Lisa?" he

asked, as they descended. He was relieved that the drive had come to an end. It had been a trying time for him. He wondered what it was all coming to? Just when the critical moment had come she had practically inhibited him from speaking. She was a strange, baffling girl, and he was helpless in her hands.

"I'm not teasing you, I simply want to finish my confessions. You must dance three dances with me, and talk to me a lot after. Perhaps I shall succeed in softening you and then you'll be more tractable. We dance till midnight. After that we sup and converse till dawn. It seems there are special complications and permissions for dancing and music in the small hours, as one's neighbours above and below are apt to want to sleep just then. Dora shirked the bother, especially as her French is so weak and her husband's worse."

They went up the stairway and were warmly welcomed by Mrs. McCook. It was a pleasant gathering of nice-looking men and pretty girls, but Paul was only half alive to it. To him it was scarcely more than a mere background for the further development of his drama. So far he took these further love-affairs of Miss Brooke as the purest make-believe, but all the same he was curiously uneasy and anxious to hear what she had in mind to tell him.

When he could talk to her again, he could discover no trace in her manner of her having lived through with him a supreme emotional moment. The softness that had given him a glimpse of infinite love, and which he had perhaps hoped might reveal itself again, was absent; in its place the old niceness and the frank friendliness of comradeship, and with them the old warning to him to stand back. She proceeded to give him the promised account of her various lovers in a light, mocking mood.

"I began very early, much earlier than your simple country maiden. My memories of childhood are rather hazy, but I should say I must have had a lover before I was out of my cradle. But I was thirteen before my heart was really moved. Since then I have been in love with so many men that I really can't remember half of them. However, I'll try and pick out those that affected me most seriously at the time. The first one was really a very nice schoolboy. His idea of love-making was to feed me incessantly with candy, which he did for a whole year till I fell a victim to the charms of another boy. The two fought. Both emerged from the combat with black eyes, which rather spoilt their beauty, and therefore killed my interest in them. It required quite an heroic effort, though, to refuse their offerings."

"And was this method of love-making as satisfying to them as it was to you?" asked Paul, beginning to be confirmed in his supposition that Miss Brooke was joking.

"Oh, we used to have clandestine meetings and we used to kiss, of course. That made me rather tired of them. They wanted to be kissing the whole time."

Paul had a momentary vertigo, though he professed by his manner to be listening in the same spirit as Miss Brooke narrated.

"The first one was always a nice boy even when he grew up and was always ready to fall in love with me again. But one fine day he got engaged, wrote to tell me about it, and asked me to congratulate him. He married. That finishes with him.

"The next interesting one was a college

man. I was about sixteen then and at the height of my musical ambition. He was musical, too, in fact quite an enthusiast. He used to pilot me about to concerts and send me tickets for the opera. Besides I was struggling then with Latin, Greek, and Conic Sections, and he used to help me polish off things —for selfish reasons, of course."

"And used you to kiss this time as well?" he asked, no longer questioning that he was hearing her personal history.

"Only at very sentimental moments," she replied, apparently overlooking the mockery in his voice. "I was older and a greater expert in emotions. One's first experiments are necessarily crude. But, to proceed, my cavalier lost his head one day and wanted me to marry him at once, which was rather absurd. So I had to give him his *congé* and accept the attentions of a less violent lover. I had always a reserve to draw upon, but so long as a man behaved nicely and didn't get altogether unreasonable, I let it accumulate. My musical friend, however, gave me some trouble. We had several stormy interviews, and at last I had positively to refuse to see him. One fine day he, too, got engaged and wrote to me asking me to congratulate him. I know he was divorced some time since, but I've completely lost sight of him."

At this moment Miss Brooke was led away to dance, but was able to join him again before very long.

"The next ⸺" were her first words, in a mock-solemn, long-drawn-out tone, as she took his arm and then she broke into laughter. "The next was a tall Southerner with nice manners, a soft voice, and a pretty way of calling me 'ma'am.' He, too, was musical— naturally, I preferred musical lovers then. The Colonel, as everybody called him, literally worshipped me, but he was as poor as a church mouse, and I used to think myself very noble to be satisfied to get stuck with him in back seats at concert-halls. He went back South after graduating, swearing he'd never forget me; but, as soon as he'd made his fortune, he was coming back to marry me. I thought that if the illusion would help him to make his fortune, he might as well keep it. In any case I should have given him cause to be grateful to me. He wrote to me half-a-dozen times, then there was a break of some months; and, when I had almost forgotten him, one fine day I got a letter from him."

"Announcing his engagement and asking you to congratulate him," said Paul, with bitterness.

"Yes. I think you may take that for granted. It is what they all do. Is it any use my telling you more? I'm beginning to think the recital is getting monotonous. And then there are some coming along and I can't remember the exact order, which came before which."

She seemed to hurry over her last words as though impatient to be done, and wearied and bored by the memory of all these dallyings with sentiment. The mocking merriment appeared also to have died out of her face and voice. She gazed idly at the dancers who, in the restricted space, almost constantly brushed up against them as they stood pressed close to the wall. Paul wondered if he were looking haggard. The air of careless merriment he had at first forced himself to assume had given way, as he listened, to a sort of nervous apathy. The one great passion of hers she had confided to him had drawn him closer to her by its intrinsic dignity. It had appealed to his finer nature, stirring it to its very depths. But these later revelations of hers revolted him by their very pettiness. What had her parents been at that such a girl had been allowed to run wild in that fashion? It was monstrous she had not been supervised and prevented from stooping to these foolish and frivolous relations with foolish and frivolous men—men she had allowed to kiss her lips!

The pang that tore him at the image revealed to him how powerless he was. He glanced at her again as she stood at his side. There was a half-sad expression now on her face, which had resumed all its babyishness again. The lock of hair near her ear lay about in a dainty twist. Her lips showed innocent and red. To kiss them *he* would lay down his life!

He was shaken; he wanted to sob aloud. But he was at a festive gathering. Round, round, up and down the room went the dancers, shuffling forward with their rapid glide, the men bending their long, supple bodies, the flowing curves of the women's dresses imparting a greater grace to the movement. The whole scene was dreamy to him. His inner thought was the only reality.

Why had she told him, why had she told him? he moaned within himself. Then as he saw a new softness appear in her face, a gleam of comfort came to him. Perhaps it had been from motives of conscience and she really repented all; perhaps, too, she had thought it right to tell him everything before allowing him to ask her to be his.

He would overlook all those episodes if only she would be his. If even they had been more serious, if even she had been a dishonoured woman, he knew now he would have had no strength not to condone. If any one had told him a year ago that he—Paul—would one day be both willing and eager to make such concessions as regards the past of a woman he contemplated making his wife, he would have denied the statement indignantly as a libel on himself.

She turned suddenly, and their looks met. Her face lighted up with a smile. "Come, Paul, it's your turn now?"

"My turn!" he echoed, her words for the moment startlingly sounding like an invitation to take his place in the procession of her lovers.

"Yes," she said. "Who was your sweetheart after the gardener's daughter?"

He denied any further love, though hating to tell the lie. But Miss Brooke persisted, entreating, provoking, urging, coaxing, pouting; subtly transforming herself into the child with its lovable moods and movements; enslaving him, rendering him powerless at her will, with this one strange exception—he could be strong enough to withhold from her the episode he was ashamed of.

"Paul, Paul," she said sternly. "Tell the truth. Are you not in love now?"

He scarcely dared look at her. He was conscious of that lock again and of another on her forehead.

"Silence betrays. Did you come to Paris for the sake of your architecture or to be near me?"

"To be near you, Lisa," he breathed.

CHAPTER VII.

ALTHOUGH the thought of Lisa's old flirtations obtruded and pricked occasionally, Paul went about the next morning in a state of subdued happiness. A wonderful calm had come over him, disturbed only at the moments when he had to thrust from him those images of other men kissing Lisa's lips. Those meaningless loves had been long dead, he argued, and, since she had made the confession voluntarily at the risk of estranging his love, it would be unfair to her for him to dwell upon them now.

At the same time he could never have conceived the possibility of such a line of argument on his part in the days before he had met Miss Brooke. Love had, indeed, set at naught all the principles he had thought to abide by—had made him yield his demand for that absolute soul-virginity he had deemed the very basis of his choice.

But away with all that now! Her love for him was, of a surety, the first that had come into her life since her great sorrow. As for Pemberton, there had never been the slightest sentiment between her and him. No doubt the fellow would now take a suitable place in the background of their life, and they would welcome him as an acquaintance. Why should he bear the man animosity?

He could not do any work that morning, but strolled hither and thither, getting joyous impressions from the sun-lit city. Lisa had not only promised to dine in the evening at the Café Pousset and afterwards to go with him to see a melodrama at the Ambigu, most of the other theatres having closed their doors, but she had given him permission to take his holiday at Perros-Guirec during the whole two months of her stay there, so that he would be virtually one of the party. The immediate outlook was, therefore, very agreeable.

He returned to the *maison meublée* where his quarters were, immediately after his midday meal, and passed the afternoon packing away his luggage, which occupation gave him the pleasurable feeling that his preparations for the happy time to come were in full swing. He sang and whistled as he worked, his overflowing vigour manifesting itself in the bold ornamental letters with which he made out the labels for his trunks: "Middleton, Paris à Perros-Guirec." At half-past five he began to think of taking a stroll before dinner, and was on the point of doing so when the *concierge* brought him up a letter with the characteristic explanation that it had come in the morning, shortly after monsieur had gone out, and that he had forgotten about it as monsieur passed by before.

Paul recognised his mother's writing, and stayed to read it. At first it did not seem to contain anything of special importance, covering much the same ground as many of its predecessors, and dealing with one or two business matters. On the third page came a reproach that he had allowed three weeks go by without writing.

"I can understand," continued his mother, "that all those hours of engrossing work every day must leave you quite fatigued, my poor child. But surely I am very reasonable in my demands, and one letter a week is not such a very heavy tax on you. Are you sure you are not overworking yourself, dear Paul? You were always a delicate child, and you are certainly not strong enough to go on living in a French hotel, with only strangers to look after you. Don't you think you ought to take a long holiday now? I am going to take Celia to Dieppe—it has all been decided and arranged to-day. The poor child has been worried and fretting and poorly for a long time past, and sadly needs this entire change of scene. Now suppose, dear Paul, you come and join us at Dieppe. You will be near to me, and I can look after you again, if only for a couple of months. We shall be starting the day after to-morrow, and we shall be staying at the Hôtel de Paris. Write to me, dear Paul, direct there, or, better still, come down and surprise us. Celia, I am sure, will be *delighted* to see you. I never understood what happened between you two exactly. You said 'good-bye' so stiffly that I made sure you had quarrelled, though Celia assures me that was not so. She is a dear, good girl, and I love her as if she were my own daughter."

Of course he couldn't go. What a bother to have to refuse! Why had they just fixed on Dieppe when they might have gone to Norway or taken a jaunt up to Scotland! And then, too, confound it! they might even make a descent upon him at Perros-Guirec, for he would have to tell his mother that was the place where he had already arranged to spend his holiday with friends. He must discuss the matter with Lisa before replying to her or telling her of his intended marriage.

But he had scarcely time to digest the letter before the man brought him up another which the postman had just left. This time the writing was Lisa's. What could she have to write to him about if it were not to postpone the evening's engagement? His nervous fingers tore at the envelope.

"DEAR PAUL.—Please don't come for me this evening, and, indeed, you must never come for me again. In writing this I am acting the part of a very good friend to you, and it is as a very good friend I should like you to remember me, as I shall always remember you.—Yours sincerely,

"ELIZABETH BROOKE."

So all was over! Behind the simplicity of the words he perceived a terrible inexorableness. If only she had signed "Lisa," it would not have crushed him so much; but the "Elizabeth Brooke" was paralyzing.

When his hand was steady enough, he wrote :—

"DEAR LISA :—Need I say your note has quite stunned me? Won't you give me a word of explanation? PAUL."

The concierge's boy delivered this at Miss Brooke's *pension*.

He scarcely knew how he got through the night. Every now and again he woke up and tossed about; and when he did lose consciousness, he had a sense of a grey infinity in which there was a great chasm. He wanted to rush to it to close it up, but was held back by some strange power.

The morning's post brought him Miss Brooke's reply.

"Dear Paul.—I am glad your letter is so sensible and to the point. Of course I owe you an explanation, but I want you not to insist on it, because I fear it will hurt you too much. The pain it would give me I deserve.—Yours, Lisa."

He found this note infinitely softer than the first and was encouraged to write again.

"DEAR LISA.—I am not strong enough to face the punishment unless I know my sin. The pain of listening to you can be nothing to the pain of this horrible gap in my mind. Won't you let me see you—for the last time? Remember it is only a day since you told me you loved me. Don't refuse. PAUL."

To which came the reply by his own messenger.

"DEAR PAUL.—Come this evening at eight and you will find me alone.—Yours,

"LISA."

All day long he nerved himself for the interview. He would rehearse nothing, anticipate nothing. When the time came, he would speak straight from his heart. Perhaps he might yet move her.

CHAPTER VIII.

Miss Brooke received him with the same cheery frankness as of yore, gave him a quick hand-shake, and installed him in his old place on the knobby-springed ottoman beneath the hanging book-shelves. The little table was laid, as usual, for after-dinner coffee, and the small copper kettle was boiling over a spirit-lamp. She was the first to speak.

"You were right, Paul. I have been thinking a good deal, and I have come to agree with you that we ought to have a last talk together. I am sensible that I am a thoroughly unscrupulous person—please don't contradict me, I mean it in sober earnest—but I am not without my redeeming moments, and so it happens I feel I ought to make my apology to you before we part. Apology! That is a very weak word to use after my immoral behaviour towards you. I mean to talk to you very openly, in fact, I am going to confess the whole extent of my misconduct. Only I want you to believe that to do so will hurt me if possible even more than you. I really do want your sympathy very badly, Paul, although I know I don't deserve it."

Her beautiful face was grave, and her voice a shade anxious. In her eyes was an expression of sincerity that compelled acceptance.

"I know you will make me understand everything, Lisa," he said.

"You must withhold your judgment till I have finished. I am going to be absolutely candid, though I am not sure whether I have ever succeeded in telling the truth about things, the whole truth, and nothing but the truth, even to myself. One shrinks from laying bare the causes and motives of one's thoughts and conduct, even when no other eye is looking. But I should feel myself quite vile now if I concealed the least thing from you."

"One can over-accentuate the baseness of one's motives as well as cover it up," he suggested.

"It is very kind of you, Paul, to try and spare me. But please save up your mercy; I warn you I shall be sadly in need of it later on. To come to facts now, Paul, I have tried to victimise you from the beginning. I have dissembled and told you lies throughout. I have systematically acted a part. I have never loved you."

He tried to make some articulation, but

not a muscle moved. He sat as if turned to stone.

"That first evening we met I knew I had turned your head, and I could see at once you were inexperienced with women as surely as if the fact had been branded upon you. I had heard somebody point you out and say you were worth fifteen thousand pounds a year, and, as afterwards you yourself told me you were rich, any doubt I might have had on the point was removed. My own poverty had just been painfully brought home to me, for I had been forced to leave Paris for want of money at the very moment my ambition began to look reasonable. I was feeling particularly bitter about it as there was no certainty at all of my being able to come back here. Poppa's savings had all gone in starting me with a good stock of dresses and keeping me here two years. He had hoped to be able to do more for me, but he could only send me my passage-money. Fifteen or even ten thousand pounds a year is a great temptation to a poor girl. Chance had never yet thrown in my way a really rich suitor, and there was I, at the moment of meeting him, almost on the eve of departure, with very little money in my pocket and indebted to the kindness of a lady for her invitation to stay the month in London. She had taken my room for me as she could not accommodate me at her own house. You see how poor I was! I set myself puzzling in the coolest possible way as to how I could get you. Instinct as well as the ease with which I had bewitched you told me there were romantic possibilities in you, of which you had scarcely any suspicion and which might easily be played upon. And a plan formed at once in my mind in the ultimate success of which I had the fullest confidence. To put the idea into your head that we meet again here in a year's time was to appeal to your romantic side. That is why I mentioned the Beaux Arts to you—your love for architecture made my game easy. I was now determined that nothing should stand in the way of my returning to Paris, that poppa somehow must raise the necessary money—even if he ran into debt. Happily he was able to send me back and to see his way clear to keep me going as long as I chose to stay."

Miss Brooke paused a moment and poured out Paul's coffee, which, however, he let stand untouched.

"Everything turned out just as I had calculated," she continued, after taking a sip at her own. "You had carried me in your mind the whole time, and you had been waiting for me and counting on my coming. So far I was delighted. For a time all went smoothly.

You were mine completely. But then an unforeseen force began suddenly to act on the position. My old enthusiasm for my work came back, and with it my old mad ambitions. Do you know what first gave me those mad ambitions? You shall hear in a moment. Anyway, my old intolerance against anything like dependence rose up in me. I wanted to make a great name and a great deal of money, all by myself. A picture by a great master—we admired it together at the salon—had just sold for thirty thousand dollars, and that inflamed me. No woman painter has yet existed of absolutely the first rank; one and all have been influenced, more or less, by a man. I wanted to be the first woman whose work should be absolutely great, absolutely original. I wanted the honour for America, for I am proud of being an American woman. But you were on the spot, and I had only to move my little finger to get you. You were an eternal temptation. Don't you think I knew you were jealous of Charlie? He has been in love with me ever since I first came here; but, poor devil, he only just manages to get along, and is only too glad if he's not behindhand with his studio rent. The reason I allowed him to hang round so much was partly because he had become a habit of mine, and partly to help me not to be tempted to give you too much of my company.

"I really wanted to fight against the temptation of your money, but more for my own sake than yours. In the first place I did not love you. And in the second, I could read your nature like a book. Your ideas and mine would never go together. I wanted a husband who would be content with such moments of love as I could spare him out of my career; to whom I could go for love when I wanted love; who would be content to live out his own life and leave me to work out mine. I do not want to be kept by my husband—rather than that I should prefer to keep him. All my rooted independence had sprung up as by magic the moment I took up my brush and palette again and looked at the model. Your notions were far too primitive for me. You would have allowed me to go on with my art as a concession—to do credit to your name, perhaps. You would have looked upon my pictures as sacred, to be hung in your house and worshipped by you before your guests; I should have wanted to sell them, to convert them into dollars.

"Do you wonder now I was strong enough to hesitate? I was only too glad when Dora said she was going to carry me off to Perros-Guirec. It would take me away from you and—temptation. Then you sent me those flowers. I was touched. Not by the flowers, but by the train of thought they set going. The ghost of my conscience came up, suggesting I should be treating you badly, seeing 'you had 'em so bad.' And then you had, say, ten thousand pounds a year! That, I suppose, had something to do with the rising of the phantom. So I determined to take you to Dora's—of course, she replied at once she would be pleased to welcome you—and I made up my mind, half to amuse myself, that I would make you propose in the cab on the way to her. I could read you through and through, and knew your every thought. So far I had kept you at a perceptible distance, now it pleased me to draw you close to me, and to see you obey without my uttering a single word of command. I told you about my old engagement just then because it gave me a sensation of daring. I calculated on stirring the romance and chivalry in you still more deeply. The experiment was risky—but it succeeded. You responded like a good ship to its helm. Then for the first time since I had known you, Paul, I suffered remorse—real remorse. Why it came just then I have never been able to make out, but all of a sudden I was dreadfully sorry for you.

"I saw clearly that even if I *had* loved you, our lives could never harmonise; that after the first honeymoon cooings, the conflict of wills and ideas would inevitably set in, and we should both be utterly and hopelessly miserable. But I did *not* love you, and I felt myself in a terrible dilemma. You were on the point of speaking, and the only thing I could think of to stop you, and to stop you for always, was to tell you my early flirtations. I was hoping to play on your prejudices and set you against me. I was true to myself then; I was throwing away—how many thousands a year?

"But I caused you suffering to no purpose, and, as I realised nothing would make you desist, the temptation of all those thousands came upon me again. I argued I was the stronger personality of the two, and I should be able to manage you—easily. Curious how I accentuated the 'easily,' and twisted my arguments to suit it. There was little to do—I just pulled the wire and the puppet worked. You'll forgive me for calling you a puppet, Paul, but you were one, you know.

"Perhaps now you will begin to understand how I felt the next morning. I really liked you, Paul, and I had done you so great a wrong from the very moment of our first meeting. I had not cried for more than three years, Paul, but I cried then. The situation was desperate, and there was nothing for it but to apply a desperate remedy.

"I have not told you all. I have purposely kept back something to the end. If I had mingled it with the rest it would have been lost, and as it is my only claim on your sympathy, I have kept it for use by itself. It is unfortunate that even here I have to begin with the confession of another lie, but I have already confessed to so many, I am hoping that one more won't make me sink any lower in your estimation. Besides, my motive in telling it was good. I refer to my old engagement. The fact was true, but the details I gave you were false. I had intended telling you the truth, but somehow it stuck on my lips. I felt I ought never to have used so sacred an experience for such a purpose. I *had* to invent a lie as I went on. But I cut it as short as I could.

"I did love the man as, it seemed to me, no woman could have loved a man before. He was almost penniless, but I did not mind that. I would have married him, and he would not have interfered with my ambitions. He would have been content to have me live away from him whilst I worked according to my own spirit, and developed the gifts he was the first to discover in me. For he was a painter, too; had starved to get a training in Europe, had starved while getting it. To help us get a start I was content at first to absorb myself in his work. That was a fatal mistake. I can scarcely trace out how it came about—and to linger on it makes me suffer terribly—but with the lapse of time I ceased to exist for him as a creature of flesh and blood. I suddenly realised that I had become a mere inspiration to him—it was only the artist in me he worshipped. All his heart and soul went into his work—he was no longer a man, but a mere mind wielding a brush. I can see him how absorbed before his canvas, tall and thin, with his scholar's stoop—for Nesbit *was* a scholar! But it had to end at last. I cried bitterly for many a night after. I had a letter from him one fine day——"

"Announcing his engagement and asking you to congratulate him?" broke from Paul's lips. His eyes were too dry for tears.

"It is the only letter of his I haven't burnt. He is famous now, but the first picture he ever sold went to buy my turquoise necklace to match the comb I had from my mother. His example was a noble one—the first picture I am offered money for shall go to poppa instead. But he would never take the gift back, and now I value it as his. It has always given me great joy to wear it—in fact, that is my one great joy apart from my work."

"You still love him! You have loved him all through!" cried Paul.

Her face softened. "You see I have quite an extraordinary vein of sentiment in me. I am not sure whether I am not ashamed of it."

"Tell me, Lisa—if I may still call you

Lisa—all those flirtations you told me about were true?"

"What a quaint question! You haven't drunk your coffee." He gulped down the cold contents of the tiny cup at one draught, for his mouth was parched.

"They all happened just as I told you, and I haven't told you a quarter."

"And do you mind my asking you another quaint question? Have you and Charlie ever kissed?"

"I have always liked to have nice men kiss me. It is a mania with me, and I shall go on doing so till the end of the chapter."

"All the same, Lisa, I love you still. Is there no hope for me? I have no prejudices. I want you, Lisa, just as you are. Your life shall be perfectly free—your career your own."

"You are good, Paul, and I have played

with you precisely as a cat plays with a mouse. You will have observed I have a good deal of the cat in me. Believe me, I am in earnest when I say I am quite unworthy of your love——"

"No, Lisa," he began.

"Listen, Paul. I want you to understand how much I love my lost darling. If he were to leave his wife and child, now and come to me and say he loved me, I would go with him to the end of the earth. No, no, Paul. My hope is only in my work. I know I shall realise my ambition. Some day you will marry a better woman than I am. And if," she continued, with a smile, "you care to write and let me know, be sure I shall congratulate you right heartily. Now tell me I have your sympathy, and then let us say good-bye."

"I love you, Lisa. Is that not sufficient

proof of my sympathy? I shall leave Paris to-night."

"Come, Paul, kiss me! For the first time and last!"

He brushed her lips so lightly that he scarce had the consciousness of doing so; then he staggered from the room.

CHAPTER IX.

He wandered he knew not whither, penetrating into strange, silent regions his foot had never trod. At the end of an hour he found he had taken a long circuit round, and that he had arrived again at the *hôtel* where Lisa lived. He crossed the narrow street, and, standing in the shadow, looked up at the window he knew so well. It stood wide open, and he could see the white ceiling of the lighted room, with the huge Japanese umbrella making a glare of colour against it. In the balcony sat two figures full in the light that flooded out. One was Miss Brooke, the other a stalwart young man in a Norfolk suit he could not recollect having seen before. A vague sound of their cheerful talking came down to him.

He turned away with a sigh, and strode rapidly to his lodging. He lighted his lamp, and, sinking into a chair, sat looking at his trunks. The labels with their bold ornamental lettering—"Middleton, Paris à Perros-Guirec"—stared him mockingly in the face. He averted his eyes, instinctively seeking in his pocket for his mother's letter, which he had till now forgotten, and was surprised to find it rolled into a ball. Smoothing it out, he read it through again.

"Write to me, dear Paul, direct there, or, better still, come down and surprise us. Celia, I am sure, will be *delighted* to see you. I never understood what happened between you two exactly. You said 'goodbye' so stiffly that I made sure you had quarrelled, though Celia assures me that it was not so. She is a dear, good girl, and I love her as if she were my own daughter."

And with these words he seemed to read the inevitableness of his fate. His rebellion against it was over. He had broken loose from the maternal leading-strings, but had made a miserable failure without them. Now he would help to fix them on him again.

The millionaire's daughter, the keynote of whose character had struck him as a charming, simple frankness, and in pursuit of whom he had set out, had proved to be a more complex specimen of womanhood than he could have imagined to exist, the very essence of that femininity of which he had always had an instinctive distrust. Celia was not brilliant, but she was safe— he knew her well enough to be sure of that.

He seized a small brush and inked over the flamboyant "Perros-Guirec," writing over the black strip the word "Dieppe" in the plainest of lettering. Then, finishing what little packing there remained to be done, he went out to consult a time-table at a neighbouring café, where he wrote and posted a note to his professor, and another to the *massier* of his class. He next hailed a cab at the rank, and the concierge carried down his trunks. "*À la gare St. Lazare!*"

The *cocher* cracked his whip, and Paul, lost in thought, was only vaguely conscious of the streets and boulevards that had become so dear to him.

THE END.

www.ingramcontent.com/pod-product-compliance
Lightning Source LLC
Chambersburg PA
CBHW030314170426
43202CB00009B/995